Table of Contents

12: Let's Wrap This Book Up!

The Work Book

Acknowledgements

I want to take the time to acknowledge my husband
Ricky Palmer. The only person in my life who have
ALWAYS believed in me. Through my failures
and victories, he has been here cheering me on.
Thank you for believing in me when the world
didn't.

-xoxo Arasi

1.

The Top-secret Answer

I'm going to let you in on a secret. Ok, Bring your ear a little closer or in this case your eyes even.

Are you ready? Are you listening?

So, the secret to starting a hair business is just to start! I know you were expecting some top-secret answer but that's the true secret most people don't tell you. Now before you stop reading or taking me seriously, hear me out. It will be well worth it by the end of this book I promise. I know you may be thinking you have to buy all these books and research until you pass out but that isn't the case necessary. Yes, research is important, but experience is more important. The only way to gain experience is to just start. The important thing to keep in mind as well is that there is no perfect time to start, if you're waiting on that the time will never come honestly.

The journey to becoming an entrepreneur is challenging and can often look like this...

But instead, most people think it looks like this and they couldn't be more wrong.

It sucks, but you are most likely going to fail several times before you get it right and that's just the truth. This day in time people don't want to share their failures so it looks like they have it all figured out.

Every time you fail you will learn what not to do. You will learn what works and what doesn't work and that's the beauty of the process. It will take time whether you believe you have it all figured out or not. Don't be discouraged by failures. I've failed plenty of times, but I didn't give up. Now you're reading this book written by me that's now published on Amazon for people to read all over the world.

Fail hard, fail fast and get back up and keep going. Every successful person has failed more times than you can imagine…

I know what some of you may be thinking... Cool, but what does this have to do with starting a hair business? It has everything to do with starting a hair business. Luckily with this book, I can help you avoid a lot of mistakes I've made and help guide you along your journey. I am 150% positive that you will have ALL the info you need to start your hair business after you finish reading this book in its entirety.

The question is, after you finish reading this book will you start your hair business? Or will you let all the information you consumed sit idle in your mind and never start?

Just start. Don't make excuses, just start... If you're ready to learn more about the hair industry, marketing and branding, growing your business, vendor information and even my biggest mistakes with hair business keep on reading!

Hair Business Talk

A question I get asked all the time, is how to start a hair business. With so many people starting hair businesses in what seems to be an over saturated field, it's challenging but can be done with the right components and mind set.

The Hair industry is a Multi-Billion-dollar industry, and what people fail to realize is that there is more than enough money to go around. As the industry grows it opens more and more spaces for people to join the hair game. Women from all over the world wear hair extensions for many reasons, as protective styling, to gain length, and just to boost confidence overall. Throughout this journey it's important to remember every customer isn't for everyone. People are not just buying a product, they are buying from you. They are buying the experience you provide as well. So, don't be afraid to jump into the hair game, there is more than enough to go around.

Starting a business can be a very overwhelming and challenging journey, but I have the blueprint to the hair game. In this book, I will teach you the ins and outs of the hair game and the questions you need to ask yourself to start your own business. By the end of this book you will be able to start your own profitable hair business with the snap of a finger.

Starting a hair business can be stressful especially if you don't know where to start. Even if you know where to start, one of the most challenging parts is finding a hair quality vendor. You can't find just any hair vendor, you need to find a hair vendor with quality hair and quality customer service. We will touch more on that later.

Finding a quality hair vendor is like finding a needle in a haystack, I'm sure many of us can relate. Often when people are on a vendor search for hair, they fail to realize that vendors are closer than they think. They can be found on Marketplaces, Social Media, Google etc. Vendors are normal people who have a variety of different marketplaces to sell from. For example, they can sell via Social media, their own website or even marketplaces like Amazon. Where ever the vendor of your choice is, it all boils down to one thing… Communication.

In this book, I will teach you how to communicate with hair vendors, the gist of hair vendors from different parts of the world, how to find your own vendors, and of course give you 9 tested hair vendors as promised.

The Beginning

I first became obsessed with hair extensions in high school. I wasn't allowed to wear it and I had no money to buy it but my boyfriend (Now my husband) would go buy the hair for me and throw it over my fence when my parents weren't home, so I could have it. Eventually my parents just let me wear it surprisingly. Fast forward a couple of years, it was the winter of 2013 and my husband bought me my first batch of virgin hair from our local beauty supply store for Christmas. I was so excited! I remember ombre hair was in great fashion at the time and I bleached hair for the first time to create an ombre effect. That early Christmas morning, I was on top of the world with my new virgin Brazilian hair.

Looking back on it now I realized it was a game changer for me. About two years went by and I began my quest for an amazing hair vendor. Believe me when I said I've seen the Good, Bad, and the Ugly. You wouldn't believe some of the quality of hair I received, but it all was worth it. Eventually I found several great hair vendors! I am now able to write this book for someone else to help them chase their dreams and of course save them time and money. Finding and testing hair vendors is unbelievably expensive.

If you fail to plan, you plan to fail

Every great business starts with an idea that turns into a plan. If you fail to plan, you plan to fail is truly a true statement. In this part, I will teach you how to devise the perfect planning process for your business.

With business if you are passionate about something it's less likely that you'll give up when things become challenging. Think about what you love, what you are good at and ask yourself if you can turn that passion into profit. For now, pick one thing and stick with it. (Hopefully in this case you are passionate about the hair industry)

I can't stress the importance of planning enough. Without a plan you and your future business will be all over the place. With a solid plan and action, anything is possible. Start with a pen and paper and brainstorm as many ideas as you can.

To come up with an idea for your brand, ask yourself these questions.

Question and Answer Time!

-Am I passionate about the hair industry?

-Why do I want to join the hair industry?

-What's missing from your niche and how can you fill that void?

-What makes you different from every other hair business?

-How can I stand out?

Ultimately, if you can fill a void you are already two steps ahead.

These days a lot of industries are becoming over saturated, so your main goal is to stand out. If you are no different from other brands, what will make a consumer want to spend their hard-earned money with you?

Business side of things

Keep in mind if you are starting a business be sure to handle to business side of things. Such as EIN's (Employer Identification Number), Business license, seller's permit, Sales tax Id and maybe even decide if you will form your business as a sole proprietor or LLC (Limited Liability Company) All of these things and the processes vary depending on what state/country you live in. All the info can be found on google depending on where you live.

Let's go over the difference between the two.

Sole Proprietor

With being a sole proprietor, you will be responsible for any debts or liabilities of your business. You are taxed as a self-employed individual.

Limited Liability Company (LLC)

With a Limited Liability Company, The Company itself is responsible for Business debts and liabilities. As a LLC you are taxed as sole proprietorships, partnerships, or corporations.

While both have their pros and cons, I would recommend Starting with just being a Sole Proprietor. There are a lot less costs and fewer rules and regulations. It's a lot easier to set up as well.

In Virginia where I'm from, you can easily access all these things directly online. Here, we must pay for our LLC and Business License. Your EIN is free as well as your sales tax ID. I know that when you pay for your LLC and get your EIN and sales tax ID it is available immediately and you can print it out right from your computer. I would love to go into detail on the business side of things, but I know it differs depending on where you live. Again, all the info can be found with a quick google search. I would recommend literally typing in

"How do I get my sellers permit in_____?
(insert your state)"

"How do I obtain my LLC IN _____? (insert
your state)"

2.

One Big Boat

Marketing, Branding, Target Audience and sales
are all in one boat and must be understood very
well to be successful. Let's get into it!

Target Audience+ Solving problems

First things first, you will need to figure out who
your target audience is so that you will know how
to appeal to your future customers. For those of you
that don't know, A target audience is your potential
customer, people you are trying to sell too. Your
target audience should be the base of your brand,

every decision will be based off your target audience.

Ex. if your target audience is the typical 30-year-old woman who is willing to pay a pretty penny for quality extensions, you would want to market to 30-year-old women that have a good paying job. Not just to women who are in the state of Virginia.

That's a quick way for your money to be wasted and for you to think social media marketing doesn't work. We will talk more about ads and social media marketing later in this book when we talk about growing and taking your business to the next level with social media!

Whether you see an ad on Tv or social media etc. They all appeal to some sort of emotion. Ultimately, with hair business people tend to appeal to a luxury feeling or making a woman feel beautiful or even like they are a part of an exclusive society.

Your brand doesn't have to be those typical scenarios. In fact, I encourage you to think outside the box a bit so you can stand out and not blend in. Not only do you need to appeal to your target audiences' feelings you need to solve a problem they have.

Let's go back to the 30-year-old target audience we mentioned before. Let's say she's a lawyer, nurse etc.... She won't have a lot of time so offering a precustomized wig she and throw on and be ready to go would be perfect. I could also appeal to a different target audience, the young woman who doesn't have much free money to spend on her hair so I offer affordable bundles. This might be the typical college student around 18-24 years of age. Both products solve a problem for that particular target audience.

Appealing to emotions of your target audience and solving their problems is what you need to be successful. Now that you have that figured out you will now need to brand your business based on your specific target audience.

Branding + Marketing.

Branding is another factor that could make or break your business. It is your business worth in a sense. With branding, everything is a factor, from the fonts you use, to the colors, to how you speak. Ex. Generic brand of paper towels vs. Bounty paper towels. That's branding. Determine what you want you brand to be known for and build your brand around that. Also try to determine your price range. What do you want your brand to be worth? Are you more affordable or high-end luxury? Ex. You don't want to be known for selling 25 cent cakes then the next day you are trying to sell the same cake for $25.

Determine how you want your brand to be represented. Find what tier you want to be in and stick with it.

Once you brand now it's time to market. Going back to what we talked about with appealing to emotions and solving problems, that's what your marketing should be all about. Create your ads around your target audience.

Ex. If your target audience is the 30-year-old nurse you would create content around her. It could be a video showing how quick it is to slay one of your wigs. Another thing you could do is literally show a nurse rushing to get ready for work. She pops on one of your wigs. She looks flawless and is out the door within 10 mins.

You could then run that video as a promotion on Facebook and/or Instagram and watch the results.

To wrap up this section I'll give a detailed example of a target audience. For example, my target audience like before is filled with 30-year-old women who have good paying jobs. Typically, a nurse, lawyer, etc. with them having a good paying job they will most likely be very busy. They may not have the time to spend a lot of time on their hair so I can solve that problem. I can create pre-customized wigs even clip ins since they both offer a quick style she may love. They can get salon quality results in a fraction of the time. I will be priced mid-range, not too high and not too low so I remain somewhat affordable. I will reach them by running an ad on Instagram and Facebook. The ad will be a video showing a middle-aged nurse successfully getting ready for work in less than 10 mins with the help of my wig. That ad will lead them to my sophisticated website for them to purchase from with monochromatic colors with a splash of royal blue. (We will talk about website building coming up soon.)

What problem will you solve for your target audience?

Question and Answer Time!

What is a target audience?

Who is your target Audience?

What will the name of your business be?

Will you be a budget friendly brand? or High-end luxury?

How do you want your customers to feel?

What experience do you want to create for your Customer?

What is your color scheme?

How will you market your product to generate sales and spread the word about your business?

3.

Products

You will need to decide what your product will be. There are so many options depending on who your target audience is. Let's start with the basics.

Hair Textures

There are 4 main categories of textures; Straight, Wavy, Curly and Kinky. Straight hair is the classic hair extension texture. It is low maintenance and can resemble relaxed hair depending on the origin. It offers such a sleek look and is almost always a go to texture. Body wave is a loose wave that is also low maintenance and is the typical wave. Its wave pattern often resembles a "S" Pattern. Deep wave is a tighter wave that resembles a curl. Higher maintenance but its texture is to die for. Kinky Curly or Kinky Straight both resemble natural hair but in either a blown-out texture or afro texture. All these textures are very versatile in their own way. They can all be straightened, curled, and worn in many ways. These are just a few of the different hair textures offered.

Hair Origins

Now let's get into hair origins, to name a few there is Brazilian, Peruvian, Indian, Cambodian, Malaysian and more!

Brazilian Hair is the most popular. It very soft, thick and versatile. It blends well with relaxed hair.

Peruvian Hair is courser than Indian and Brazilian hair. It is very soft and light.

Indian Hair is very fine, light and bouncy. Styles easy but can often be frizzy.

Cambodian Hair is slightly course, holds curls well and has a ton of bounce and body. It is said to be the most sought-after hair because of how thick and luxurious it is.

Closures and Frontals

First let's start with the difference between a closure and a frontal.

A closure is typically 4x4 in size. It is usually just enough space for a part or two. While a Frontal is typically 13x4 in size and give you an entire hairline worth of parting space.

Closures come in a variety of sizes. 4x4,5x5, and even 7x7! They are great for the woman who doesn't want any of her natural hair left out, but she wants a low maintenance style.

Frontals come in a variety of sizes as well 13x4,13x2, 13x6 and even 360 Frontals that cover the entire perimeter of your head. They are great the woman who wants none of her hair left out but wants a lot of versatility with her everyday styling. While frontals have a lot of perks, they are often very high maintenance which can be very expensive.

Let's get into the lace aspects.

There are many types of lace, my personal favorite is swiss lace. It is most commonly sold and worn. They also have silk-based closures, which I wouldn't recommend. They look natural but tend to not blend once installed. Lace also comes in different colors, light brown, dark brown and a recent favorite transparent lace. Lace can also be tinted to match skin colors so I would recommend starting out with transparent, beige, or light brown lace being that they are the most versatile for your customer.

Wigs

Wigs are also very popular on the market. They can be handmade, or machine made. Wigs can also be made with Frontals, lace closures, 360 frontals or even full lace. A crowd favorite is precustomized wigs since a lot of women don't know how to deal with lace so it's helpful if it comes precustomized when they receive it. People also like to order custom wigs, so if you are selling wigs it's best to have that option available for customers to build their own wigs. If you are handmaking wigs, you may have heard that spandex caps are the way to go. I personally found that using the wig caps with adjustable caps are better. It not only looks better but can be adjusted to fit any size head. I will have tutorials on my YouTube channel "The Pretty Mompreneur" If you are interested in checking that out.

Question and Answer Time!

To get a better idea of the product you will offer ask yourself these questions:

What kind of hair you will sell? Mink, Virgin, Human, Premium Blend, Synthetic, Colored hair extensions, or even extensions for natural woman of color?

What grade and density will your product be?

Will you just be selling Hair extensions, or will you expand and sell Wigs, Closures and Frontals as well?

What kind would you sell?

What Origin(s) will you sell?

What lengths will you sell?

Will you sell Bundle Deals/Packages as well?

4.

Hair Vendor Basics

Now that you know what kind of products you want to sell you will now need to find a vendor. Vendors can be overseas as well as local. You will need to figure out what works best for your brand. If you want to be a more reliable brand, I would rely on local vendors, meaning vendors in the united states. Overseas vendors aren't as reliable but if you have inventory that won't be a problem. The most important thing people don't mention is that you need to build a relationship with your vendor. Communication is key! Just a tip *

Vendors can be found anywhere. From Instagram, AliExpress, DHGate, and even Amazon. It's all about communication. If you don't know where to start, begin looking at reviews from different vendors and try out vendors within your price range. Every product has a markup, find a price range where you will be able to make a profit, but it won't be too far out of price range for your consumer. We will go into detail about vendors in part two of this book. I'll also give you 9 tested vendors!

Question and Answer Time!

Ask yourself these questions:

What is my target audience budget?

How fast do I want to be able to get my product to my customers?

What quality hair will I sell?

Who will be your hair vendor? Where will you source from?

What is my Budget?

How affordable do I want my product to be?

How much do I want to make per bundle sale?

United States Vendors

To do business with vendors from the United States, you will need a sellers permit business license. You will simply email/call the vendor and tell them you would like to do business with them and ask them how to make a purchase and their minimum order requirements.

Some vendors will ask you for a sellers permit/ business license some won't. Having one not only allows you to purchase your supplies tax free but it also shows that you are serious about your business. If you don't have one work on getting one as soon as possible being that it is required by law because you will need to pay sales tax in your state.

A way to bypass this is to shop on marketplaces such as Amazon. You won't need a sellers permit or business license to purchase using marketplaces.

Overseas/China Vendors

With purchasing from overseas, the requirements aren't as strict as purchasing in the United States.

When communicating with vendors overseas you will always want to be very educated when doing business. Never ask questions that can be found via google. The last thing you want is to be taken advantage of. The more aware and confident you are, the more respect you will gain.

Before you initiate conversation have a clear idea of how much you are willing to buy and how often. Vendors want to know what to expect when doing business with you.

Starting out you can even communicate with the vendor and let them know that you will be driving in a lot of sales on a consistent basis and a lot of them will even offer you a discount from the very beginning. The better relationship you gain and the more money you are making the bigger the discount they will offer you.

Once you've established a track record of consistent orders you can ask for net 30 payment terms. This is a form of trade credit which allows you to pay for your supplies up to 30 days later to help with your cash flow.

How to Find A Vendor

As mentioned before, the quality of hair is just as important as quality of customer service. When finding a vendor, it is crucial that they have both. Finding a quality hair vendor is one of the most challenging parts of starting a hair business. We must be able to provide quality products if we want our business to thrive.

The quickest way to find a hair vendor is to search marketplaces. Amazon, AliExpress, and DHGATE, to name a few. Believe it or not reviews are powerful… Not only do they serve a purpose to customers they help other vendors as well just like you. You can see how the quality of the hair is and the quality of customer service just by reading the reviews.

Let real people test the vendor for you! They let you know the quality of the hair, whether it sheds, tangles etc. They will also let you know the quality of customer service. If they respond quickly, ship in a timely fashion etc.

After reading reviews, you should have a pretty good idea about that vendor. Do they have quality hair? Do they have good quality customer service?

If all checks out, you're ready for the final step. Now it's time to make a purchase of your own. Test the hair fully before you sell to your customers. Color the hair, Straighten the hair, Curl the hair, Wash the hair etc. Learn the ins and outs of the hair so that you're ready to answer any questions your customer may have. This will also help you promote your hair in various ways.

It is very important to become an expert with your product. If you don't know the answers to any questions a customer may have with your product then who will? Gain Authority... How do you Gain Authority? Become an expert in the hair game, learn, study, know your product in and out.

Gain authority. Authority brings trust. Trust bring sales.

Communicating with Vendors

Communication is the task at hand, the true task at hand is building relationships. It is very important to build a relationship with your vendor, Yes, you've guessed it…. Through communication. You build relationships through communication. I know it sounds basic and like common sense, but you wouldn't believe how many people fail at communication.

When I say build relationships, I'm not talking about a personal relationship, although that may come! I'm talking about a business relationship. In business the strongest asset you have is your relationship. We all know the saying "……. It's about who you know…" In many ways that is nothing but the truth being that networking is key to any successful business. The question is, how do I communicate and build a business relationship?

First things first, I would recommend communicating through email. Why? You may ask. It shows a level of professionalism. When building a business relationship, you want to show them that you mean business so be sure to start the conversation right with email.

Now you're probably sitting with your email open but now you don't have a clue of what to say. Before we even get to what to say you need to double check and make sure you know how to write an email. Again, I know this may sound basic but it's a common mistake. Be sure you know how to properly format an email. Have a greeting, closing, etc. Also make sure you have a subject in the subject line.

Now on to the number one question. How do I communicate with a hair vendor? I've broken it down in 4 steps.

Step 1: Introduce Yourself

Tell them who you are. People like to communicate with people, meaning it's ok to let them know you are human just like they are. I think often we are afraid to approach vendors or just business people in general because we fail to realize that, they are just like us.

Step 2: State Your Purpose

Tell them why you are emailing them. Make your purpose very clear, tell them what you expect from them as a vendor and how you will be a good customer or asset to them.

Step 3. Add Value

Make sure you add value to your vendor. You want to ensure they are benefiting as well, otherwise why would they want to work with you?

Step 4: Negotiate

Negotiate pricing. Keep in mind they are in business and need to make money as well.

Step 5: Ask

Ask all questions you need. You need, to have a clear understanding of agreements, pricing etc. Make sure there is no confusion. Keep in mind, every vendor will not respond to you. Every vendor won't want to work with you. It is important to stay positive and motivated during this process because it is not an easy task.

Marketplaces to find vendors

Marketplaces are great places for you to find a vendor. I want to share of few of my favorite online marketplaces and the benefits of each of.

Let's start with Amazon

Amazon is the world's largest online retailer. They sell many things but most importantly, they sell hair extensions, wigs etc.

So many hair vendors join Amazon to sell to people all around the world, which makes this a great opportunity for you.

The biggest benefit of having a vendor on amazon is being able to use amazon prime. This is beneficial because you will be able to receive hair for your customers in two days guaranteed and sometimes you can even get it within one day! This is perfect for the person that wants to buy as they sell. If you get a bad batch for whatever reason, it's super easy to return and get your money back or just exchange.

Another one of my favorites is DHGATE, they are my favorite online marketplace. While their shipping times are higher, they provide the best quality hair in my opinion. They also offer wholesale pricing automatically. DHGATE typically have overseas vendors, which is why the shipping times are a bit higher. They also offer coupons for an additional discount. All vendors are also one message away, which is where you will communicate with them and negotiate pricing if you choose to.

They also have other marketplaces such as Alibaba and AliExpress however I don't personally use them, so I can't offer much advice on those platforms. I do know that between amazon and DHGATE you will have everything you need.

Inventory or Drop shipping.

Let's Talk sourcing. Sourcing is the way in which you find out how something can be obtained. First you will need to decide how you want to source. There are many ways to source and the most important thing is to find what works best for you and your business. The way you decide to source will have a direct impact on the way your product is packaged, shipped, the amount of time it takes you to get your product shipped etc. Let's learn some important terms.

Drop shipping

Drop shipping is a supply chain management method in which the retailer does not keep goods in stock but instead transfers the customer orders and shipment details to either the manufacturer, another retailer, or a wholesaler, who then ships the goods directly to the customer

Drop shipping is a method in which you don't keep the product on hand but instead transfer the customer's order and shipment details to the wholesaler who then ships the goods directly to the customer. Another way is to simply order the product after the customer has purchased the product then ship out to the customer with your own packaging. Drop shipping is becoming more and more popular as time goes on. This method is great for someone who doesn't have a lot of money to invest in inventory right away.

Inventory

Inventory is product you have in stock. If you have product on hand that means you have inventory. There is no set amount of hair you should have in stock. It really depends on how fast your hair sells… If it sells fast you will want to have a larger inventory. If you're just beginning, having a few bundles on hand will be fine. If you are just starting out and building inventory, 25 Bundles would be the perfect amount to have just starting off. You should have various lengths and textures in stock from 12"-26" to start off.

What is wholesale? Wholesale is the selling of goods in large quantities to be retailed by other. Often if you wholesale from your vendor you will be able to buy hair at a very discounted rate but often times you will have to pay a larger amount in advance but it's worth it because of the inventory you will obtain.

.**What is buying as you sell?** Buying as you sell is simply just that. When you sell a product on your website, then buy the product and ship it out as soon as possible. Be sure to let your customers know shipping info as to how long shipping and processing takes.

Take the time to really decide how you want to source… If you need help, ask yourself these questions.

Do you want to buy in bulk? (wholesale)

Do you want to Dropship?

Or do you want to buy as you sell?

These questions are important because it will vary your approach with the vendor.

Question and Answer Time!

What is drop shipping?

What is Inventory?

What lengths do I want to have in stock?

What textures do I want to have in stock?

How much do I need to start my inventory?

Great Tested Vendors to Start

As promised, I'm going to give you guys not one but 9 tested hair vendors you can use to start out.

Amazon

Ms. Beauty

Jinren

Golden Rule

ULOVE HAIR

2 ILING

Dhgate

Gaga Queen

Tiffany hair

Galiqueenhair no 1

Wewill Hair

5.

Where Will You Sell?

Now that you have your vendor and decided on inventory or drop shipping, you will need to decide on how you will sell. Do you want to sell online or sell in person or even both? is the question.

Marketplaces

As we mentioned before a lot of companies sell on marketplaces an that's no different for you. A lot of people think that when they start their hair business they must sell on their own and that's not true at all. Amazon, AliExpress, Dhgate etc. are all marketplaces that allow you to easily sell on their platforms. The benefit of selling on a marketplace like Amazon for example is the crazy amount of traffic your products can attract. The customers will come to you with a quick search. I've even seen companies start selling on a marketplace then brand off to start their own store. It's easy to do that once you've gained enough traffic and loyal customers who love your product! Marketplaces do have their own rules and regulations so be sure to educate yourself on that before getting started. Each platform is a little different.

Brick and Mortar Business

Brick and mortar companies can be very intimidating especially when you're just starting out. It's a big investment and could easily go downhill if your sales drop or even worse if sales never come in. The benefit of a brick and mortar business is being able to serve your local community with your product. While e commerce has become very popular there are a lot of people who still want product on demand especially if you're in the hair business. As a former hairstylist I know how women love hair on hand and often they decide to get their hair done last minute but they don't have hair extensions. This could even go back to solving problems like we mention in this book a ton of times. The advantage of having hair on hand could be that you solve the problem of women not having hair extensions when they decide they want their hair done. You don't necessarily need a brick and mortar business to sell hair on hand but if you want to be taken seriously this could be a necessity.

I know there is someone out there that may want to open a brick and mortar business, but they don't have the money or even the credit to open a brick and mortar business. I'm going to let you in on a craigslist secret you may or not know. If you go to craigslist and go to the housing section. Then office and commercial. You can then type in "Private Owner" or "Private Landlord" and if available in your area you can find spaces for rent where the landlord won't require a credit check and is often affordable. There are always ways to reach your goals, when a door closes there is always a window waiting to be opened. At www.theprettymompreneur.com we believe this wholeheartedly.

Online

Just about every business has a website, whether it's for informational purposes or e-commerce. In this part, I will teach you about website building and how to build your own in less than 30 minutes. There are a lot of e-commerce platforms. However, I personally found Big Cartel to work amazing for beginners. Everything about it is simple but gives an amazing website to work with for only $10 a month on the platinum plan. When you are ready to advance, I would recommend Shopify. Shopify gives you a lot more options and looks more professional overall for about $30 a month. YouTube offers a ton of tutorials on how to use each.

Again, Shopify is highly recommended. However, it will take a little time to get used to it if you aren't tech savvy.

It will make it a lot easier if you already have:

-product pictures

-a logo saved in PNG format

-well written product descriptions

Key Website Components

1. Big Logo – When someone visits your website your logo should be one of the first things they notice. It should always be uploaded in PNG format. PNG files have a transparent background while JPEG files have a solid background. PNG is always best for logos believe me.

2. Domain – The domain is actually one of the most important factors of your website. Your domain name is your web URL, its how

people find our website. Ex.
www.theprettymompreneur.com

With a custom domain name people will take you seriously. ALWAYS get your own domain name.

3. Slideshow – Be sure to have high quality photos for your website. I can not stress this enough. Also make sure the images are all the same size. It just helps the website flow better. These days our phones are even good enough to take quality pictures. If you don't have the budget to afford a professional photographer simply turn your phone horizontally and snap away with good lighting. Natural sunlight also is great for lighting if you don't have a professional lighting set up. Make sure the sunlight is in front of your model and behind your photographer. Once you get the great picture you can edit on your phone if you don't have photoshop or lightroom. Facetune is a great phone editing ap.

4. Email sign up – Email signups are necessary! They are great for marketing, building relationships with customers, and even great for retargeting people who didn't complete checkout.

5. Collection of Products on Home page – Be sure to showcase your best products on your homepage.

6. About and Contact Pages – People want to know who they are buying from and most importantly how to contact you if needed. Your contact Info should always be very detailed and easily found.

Website tip

#1 If you haven't heard the term SEO already believe me you will. SEO is something I really had to learn and now I can teach you! SEO stands for search engine optimization. Search engine optimization is key because it determines where you rank on google and determines your organic traffic reach. The best way to optimize your website for SEO is to make sure everything is written in great detail from your product descriptions, about page, contact page, FAQ page and even the pictures you upload. Yes, even the pictures you upload will need a description. When you google let's say, "Blue Knife' the only way google knows what the image is, is because of alt text or the description that was posted along with the image. You want everything on your website to be searchable. Searchability is key!

#2 When planning for a photoshoot it may be helpful to contact local hairstylists and makeup artists. They may be willing to collaborate with you for a lower price or even for free. Not only will be be great exposure for you but for them as well. You will be able to reach two sets of audiences you may not have been able to reach if you hadn't worked with a hairstylist or makeup artist. They will most likely promote their work after working with you and it will be free promotion!

Question and Answer Time!

If selling online, who will be your host?

What is my monthly budget for my online retail store?

Will I design it myself or hire out?

Do I want my website to be bold or simple?

6.

Money Honey

Payment

One of the most important things is obviously getting paid. There are many payment processors to use. I personally recommend PayPal, Stripe and Shopify Payments. Each has its advantages and disadvantages, you will ultimately just have to use which one works best for you and your brand. Choosing which you will use will determine how fast you get paid. With PayPal you receive payment immediately. You will be able to order a free debit card for your PayPal account which is very convenient. With Stripe there is a 7 business Day turnaround (eventually you will have a two-day turnaround) and the money earned minus Stripes fees will be sent directly to the checking account of your choice and Shopify payments has a two-day turnaround and payment will also be sent directly to your bank account. Shopify and PayPal both offer free card readers for in person sales so don't forget to take advantage of that as well.

Fraud and Chargebacks

You must be mindful of fraud to avoid issues with your payment processor so be sure to have all the proper settings in place to limit the amount of fraud activity. This day in time it's very important to keep record of all receipts, emails and tracking numbers to avoid fraud and chargebacks with customers. Chargebacks could result in Stripe, Shopify Payments and PayPal closing your account because your business is high risk. Double check and make sure that each order has a low fraud risk before accepting the payment and shipping out your customer orders. Each platform has fraud tools which is very convenient for the seller.

Business Income

When income starts to come in, I know how tempting it may be to spend it. Money is meant to be spent but it should be spent on the right things. When starting a business, it is very important that you put the money back into your BUSINESS not your POCKETS. This will allow your business to grow. You can hire an employee to help you, hire freelancers to help with flyers and graphic design work, you can invest in inventory etc. There are so many things you can spend your money on. Just please do not spend your money Chanel Bags, clothes, cars etc. Yes, you may have a new few fancy items, but your business will not grow, and it will suffer. You don't have to put every penny back into the business however, I would recommend putting 70% back into the business and keeping 30% for yourself if possible.

It's always best to have separate accounts for business and personal. It will be way easier to keep track of expenses and profits. This will especially be important for when it's time to file taxes. Yes. You MUST file taxes on your business.

Question and Answer Time!

What Payment processor works best for you?

How quick do I need to get paid?

How will you accept payment? Will you accept credit cards? Invoices? Cash? or all the above?

7.

The Customer is Always Right

Customer Service

The Customer is always right. I know what you're thinking, we just talked about fraud and customer chargebacks. How could the customer always be right?

The phrase the customer is always right is a standard of Great customer service. this means that you will go above and beyond to ensure your customer is satisfied. If you have an honest customer, the customer should always be right.

Customer service says a lot about your brand and could ultimately make or break your brand. No one wants to spend their hard-earned money on a brand with poor customer service. It's important to know that you are not just selling a product, you are also selling an experience.

Ways to have good customer service:

-Respond as quickly as possible to all inquiries. No one wants to wait days and days or even too many hours for a response. A slow response time can lead to losing a potential customer.

-ALWAYS speak to customers with the utmost respect.

-Create a memorable experience for your customer. as stated before; you are not just selling the product you are creating an experience.

-Build a relationship with your customer.

-Follow up with your customer

-offer them great tips, etc.

Question and Answer Time!

How can I keep my customer happy?

Is the customer, always right?

How can I keep a high response time to improve customer service?

How can I build a relationship with my customer?

8.

Let's Pack It Up

Packaging

Now that you have everything mapped out, you will need to figure out your packaging. When deciding your packaging keep your branding in mind. Colors, Fonts and brand standards should remain the same. Packaging will ultimately say a lot about your brand. You can either have your packaging professionally made or opt for DIY options. Remember to keep your target audience in mind when choosing your packaging as well. Make your packaging as nice as you possibly can and try to always make it an experience for your customer. How would you like to receive a package? Keep that in mind.

If you have a pretty good budget, I would recommend these companies from Instagram

@Luxe_creations__ they are a Florida based brand that makes everything from custom satin bags, bonnets, head wraps etc.

@shaynamade makes some of the most beautiful business cards I've ever seen in my life.

You can also use websites like Etsy to find professional packaging.

If you don't yet have the budget for Professional packaging, here's a few ways you can DIY your Packaging.

Bundle wraps: You can add cute pom poms, ribbon, rhinestone strips etc. all from the craft section of Walmart. You can also Print labels you type up using Microsoft Word and simply tape them on. You can also get some made from Vistaprint. Vistaprint can be your best friend trust me.

Wig Boxes: You can actually use T-shirt boxes for this. They are very affordable and clean looking. You could add some labels to personalize it. Or simply tie some pretty ribbon around the box for a personalized look if you don't have labels.

Tissue Paper: is great for making your packaging look nice

Gift bags: Gift bags offer a nice touch when a customer is coming to personally pick up an order. Gift bags can be found anywhere from the dollar store, Walmart or amazon. Find some that fit with your branding and you will be all set!

Shipping 101

Speaking of packing it up, we should go over shipping basics. Shipping used to be a scary topic for me because it was honestly something I never did before unless it was a letter and it's not too much of a difference.

The best tip I can give you is to invest in a scale. I can not stress this enough. Its so much easier and quicker to print prepaid shipping labels that it is to package your orders up and take them to the post office and wait for them to weigh each item and pay for shipping then.

This will also help you to price your shipping costs properly on your website. With prepaid shipping labels you can simply have the postman pick the packages up from your door or drop them off without all the long wait times.

Question and Answer Time!

When creating your packaging ask yourself, how would I like to receive my package?

What experience do you want to create for your customer?

How will you package your first sale? Where will you get your packaging supplies from?

9.

Social Media 101

Today, you can barely function without social media and businesses are the same way. I want to teach you key points that helped me with social media and organic traffic and growth hacks.

Instagram.

Instagram is one of my favorite platforms to build a hair business or any business really. Its so easy to access from people from all over the world literally. Instagram should definitely be one of your most used platforms. Let's get into why and how to use Instagram for business.

Hashtags and Location

Using hashtags can expose you to a ton of people and help get exposure for your brand. A lot of people also don't realize that location on a photo also helps people find them. Make sure every picture you post has a location and relevant hashtags. Avoid using huge hashtags if you don't have a huge following. When I say huge hashtags, I mean hashtags that are commonly used with a huge number. When you type a hashtag, you will be able to see how many times its been used. Its also a good idea to always use hashtags that are relevant to your area. Ex. #757hairstylist vs just #hairstylist

It is also important to note that you always need at least 3 groups of hashtags to rotate. If you constantly use the same hashtags Instagram will see you as spam.

Slide in the DM's

Don't be afraid to slide in some dm's and get to know people. You don't want to sell to them right off the bat but it's important to start building relationships especially if you direct message them from your personal page. You can let them know what you do and et them know about your business page and they may keep you in mind for when they are looking for a good product like yours. Don't be spammy or too much of a salesman. Take the time to like potential customers pictures and leave a nice comment pertaining to their picture. They will start to notice you, and this will build a relationship. Which could turn into a business relationship.

Grow your Following

The easiest tip I can give you would be to follow potential customers. The key to this is to go to your competitions pages and follow their followers. If they are following a hair company, they clearly are interested in hair extensions. If they like what you have to offer, they will stick around and potentially become a great customer! To attract ACTIVE followers, go to one of their posts and follow people who have liked the content they produced. This will be more effective if you choose posts that looks like something you may post.

-Be Consistent with your posts. People love consistency. If they constantly see you on their news feed, you are less likely to be forgotten. But DON'T Spam. You can even have followers that will regularly check for your posts but if you don't have a set schedule, how will they know when to check for your posts?

Don't bombard your followers with price lists

No one wants to feel like they are constantly being sold to. The truth is, when someone really wants your product they will just go to your website and buy it. They don't need a constant reminder of your prices.

Create engaging content for your business page.

Ask questions, give tips, show mini tutorials. Your followers want to benefit from your content as well.

Be sure to snag up as many testimonials as you possibly can.

People want to know that people enjoy your product. It builds trust and they will feel more comfortable to shop with you.

Always respond to your followers' comments.

Always remember that your followers are real people and they want a response. Imagine giving someone a compliment and they say nothing back… ouch!

Post content your followers can relate too

This goes back to appealing to emotions

If you don't use Instagram Analytics you are missing out. It will give you all the stats of your followers, track your engagement and even tell you when your peak times to post are based on when your followers are active. To use Instagram Analytics all you must do is change the Instagram account to a business account and link it to your Facebook Page. If you've been using ads you should be aware of this on Instagram.

YouTube is your secret weapon

YouTube is the number one place people go to when deciding to try out a new brand so make sure you are up there! If you don't have money to pay a youtuber or product to send them for free consider starting your own brand channel where you show your potential customers how to use your product. Luxy Hair on YouTube is a great example of what to do with a branded hair channel. People will be able to see the quality of your hair and be able to learn how to care for the hair and style the product. The possibilities are endless!

Pinterest for the Win

Lot of people don't understand the power if Pinterest for business. It can grow so much traffic to your website if done correctly. Posting gorgeous selfies wearing your hair, customer selfies etc. can direct people right to your website and could even give you more sales.

Blog your heart out

Speaking of Pinterest, once they click on your beautiful selfie it would great for the picture to not just direct them to your website once they click the link but a helpful post. This post could be anything that would help the customer. Ex. How to wash your hair extensions, how to make wand curls stay for days, how to turn old extensions into a wig, how to bring old extensions back to life etc. Not only is this helpful to the client. It will help you gain authority and build trust with your customer. This will also help with your SEO and help you rank better with Google. This is a great example of Organic traffic which is the opposite of paid traffic.

10.

The Launch

Now that you have everything together it's time for you to prepare to launch! I can't stress enough the importance of a great launch. You need to build anticipation for your brand. before you even launch your website.

Plan your launch out and promote heavy to family members, friends, social media and even paid advertising. Start your brand with a strong launch and keep the momentum going!

The Planning

The first thing you should do is start to plan out your launch. Write down your ideas, goals and devise a plan.

Your end goal is the most important because it will help you map out the steps you need to take to reach that goal. Everyone has a different end goal. Your end goal may be to grow an audience to 5 k on social media and have at least 50 sales and 10 great reviews launch day. While someone else's end goal may be to just get one sale and have 50 followers via social media. No end goal is wrong, it just depends on what you want.

Influencers

Influencers can have such a big impact on not only your launch, but your overall business Influencers usually have a big following and not only do they have a huge following their followers trust them. When you contact an influencer to promote your brand you are asking them to introduce and represent a product to their customers. Be sure you have a quality product so that when the customer buys your product off the strength of the influencer, they are not disappointed. They could then become a lifetime customer. Even if you are no longer working with the influencer, they will still be a customer of yours.

Influencer marketing is highly highly recommended and could put your business on a new level if you work with the right one.

Before working with an influencer ask to see their analytics. This will show you where their followers are from, their men to women follower ratio. And their best times to post. Looking into this information can make things a breeze for you and help you make the best decisions.

You also want to work with influencers that have a high engagement. This will help you avoid fake influencers with a high number of ghost followers or even fake followers.

How I would Launch

You may be thinking... well how do I launch? Here's how I would launch.

Let's stick with the same 30-year-old woman with the great job.

First, I'd reach out to influencers in that age group. You can find influencers on Instagram, Facebook, YouTube. Influencers are people with an audience (followers). It's best to find influencers with a very engaged following meaning that their followers' comment and like their photos or posts and its also important that they interact with their followers as well. Many will ask for payment in exchange for promotion, some will just ask for the free product in exchange for promotion and some will want payment and the free product. Most people will decline if you offer them a "discounted price" for your product in exchange for promotion. I would never recommend that.

I would also create great content showing how my product could solve a problem. (lack of time so I create an easy to wear wig and I show how easy it is to put it on) I would also create content on how it's used, stored, maintenance, styling etc...

I would then use the content I created to run an ad on Facebook and IG targeting my target audience to bring awareness to my launch and overall brand. The description would include the launch date and any other helpful info.

I could also do a giveaway. Giveaways are great for getting people to engage with our content, build your email list, following and get people familiar with your product!

To do a giveaway, first decide what you want them to give you in exchange for what you will give them. This could be a follow, subscribe, an email or even a shout out. Let's go into more detail. You may want more followers for your Instagram page, Subscribers for your YouTube channel, more emails so you can grow your email list, or more exposure so a shout out would come in handy from multiple people for your giveaway.

Make sure your giveaway benefits not only you but your audience as well. Also be mindful that giveaways can also attract the wrong crowd... Meaning people who don't care about you or your brand and they just want the free stuff.

Ads

Speaking of Ads, Let's talk about them.

You will want to run ads if it fits within your budget and it's crucial that you make it fit into our budget even if its only $5 a week.

Business revolves around attention. The more attention you have the more potential customers, more exposure, and of course more money! And vise versa without attention there's no money. No money equals no business. Always put your brand in front of as many people as you possibly can.

The most popular places o run ads would be Facebook Google Ads and Instagram. However, I found Facebook and Instagram to be the most lucrative platforms to use for paid advertising.

Times are changing and its pretty obvious majority of people spend most of their time on social media than anywhere else. People even spend more time watching YouTube than regular Television these days. I'm guilty of that as well. So that's where you should be advertising!

Let's talk about how to run an ad.

To run an ad on Facebook and Instagram you must have a business page on Facebook. This business page will link to your Instagram page once you've switched from a personal to business account on Instagram. You can now run ads easily on Instagram and Facebook! You can choose to promote any of the posts you have on your Instagram feed if it follows Instagram's guidelines. You can decide who you want to advertise to with just a few clicks. Remember to promote to your target audience like we discussed before. The only downside in my opinion is just that. I know that sometimes I personally wanted to create a post special for advertising, but I didn't want it on my feed necessarily. That's something to keep in mind when deciding what to promote.

11.

The Successful Business

Staying Organized

As your business grows, you may notice that it is becoming harder to stay organized. Lack of organization could cause your customer service to decrease and even worse could cause your business to go downhill.

To stay organized with your customers emails, messages etc. I would recommend having a business email. You can get one through Microsoft and even Gmail. This will help you to stay organized and make it easier to respond to all emails.

To stay organized with Social media, I would come up with a set schedule. A set schedule to engage with your social media followers and respond to comments and respond to Direct messages. The last thing you want is to be known for the brand that never responds and has poor communication.

To stay organized with orders, I would print every order and keep it neatly filed away that way you always have track of every order in case you need to refer to a specific order for a return, issue etc.

To stay organized with actual orders, I would have bins for Outgoing orders, Incoming inventory, and returns. This way you can keep track of things that need to be shipped out and things that were possibly returned. This is crucial because the worst thing is getting a complaint about an order never being shipped or shipped late because the package was somewhere stuck beside your desk.

The Scale

I mentioned before to always try to put at least 70% back into your business to help grow. Now that your seeing income come in and you can judge your profit, it may be a good time to scale and grown bigger.

Now may be the time to hire the assistant to ship out your packages, keep track of customer emails, and even package orders. You may want to do a huge campaign, but you need nice graphics, so you hire a graphic designer. You may need a website upgrade where you need to hire a web designer and a photographer for a professional shoot etc.

Now isn't the time to make bad decisions it's the time to let your money work for you and scale your business to the next level! Evaluate what your business needs and grow.

Now would also be the best time to spend as much money as you can with your advertising and reach even more people. You could even hire brand ambassadors to represent your brand and bring in even more loyal customers.

Its time to scale and reach new heights!

The Mindset

Once you have your business up and running the most important thing you can do is keep your business going and growing. Consistency is key. Everything you do has to be consistent, from posting on a regular schedule to doing daily tasks for your business. If you are consistent, dedicated and focused you will be able to keep your business afloat even when things get rough. Be sure to always set goals and standards for you brand and work diligently each day. Starting a business isn't easy but it's rewarding and worth it. The most important thing is to not give up and always believe in yourself. The sky is the limit, and anything can be achieved with hard work and determination. You are never limited. Your work ethic must match your dreams.

12.

Let's Wrap this book up!

As mentioned before marketing and branding plays a major role in the success of your business. If you don't have any marketing experience, I would highly advise that you gain knowledge in that area. Learn how to optimize your website for search engines (SEO). Also learn how to run promotions and advertise on social media. Hire Influencers on Social media platforms to help spread the word about your product. Don't be afraid to give product away for free. You must keep in mind that no one knows your brand or who you are, you have to be willing to hustle, hustle, hustle. It will pay off in the end if you are consistent. You must invest in yourself and your business 125% to keep it afloat. Stay consistent, work hard and just believe in yourself. Remember that anything is possible especially with proper planning and dedication. Good Luck on your Hair Business! We've now reached the end of this book and I hope you were able to learn how to start your own hair business with the information provided. I wish you all the best of luck on your journeys! Be sure to leave a review on amazon, share with friends and let me know if this helped you on your journey!

-xoxo Arasi

If you would like to join a community where you can learn more tips and tricks like the ones mentioned in this book be sure to follow me on social media and follow my blog. You won't want to miss out!

Blog: www.theprettymompreneur.com

Instagram: @arasipalmer

Pinterest: The Pretty Mompreneur

YouTube: The Pretty Mompreneur

Question and Answer Time!

How will you maintain your business and grow?

How can you stay motivated?

Work Book

This section is for our boss babes that would like a special place to answer the questions. If you have the eBook version of this, you can print out these pages to write out your answer. If you have the paperback version feel free to write directly in this space!

-Am I passionate about the hair industry?

-Why do I want to join the hair industry?

-What's missing from your niche and how can you fill that void?

-What makes you different from every other hair business?

-How can I stand out?

What is a target audience?

Who is your target Audience?

What will the name of your business be?

Will you be a budget friendly brand? or High-end luxury?

How do you want your customers to feel?

What experience do you want to create for your Customer?

What is your color scheme?

How will you market your product to generate sales and spread the word about your business?

What kind of hair you will sell? Mink, Virgin, Human, Premium Blend, Synthetic, Colored hair extensions, or even extensions for natural woman of color?

What grade and density will your product be?

Will you just be selling Hair extensions, or will you expand and sell Wigs, Closures and Frontals as well?

What kind would you sell?

What Origin(s) will you sell?

What lengths will you sell?

Will you sell Bundle Deals/Packages as well?

What is my target audience budget?

How fast do I want to be able to get my product to my customers?

What quality hair will I sell?

Who will be your hair vendor? Where will you source from?

What is my Budget?

How affordable do I want my product to be?

How much do I want to make per bundle sale?

What is drop shipping?

What is Inventory?

What lengths do I want to have in stock?

What textures do I want to have in stock?

How much do I need to start my inventory?

If selling online, who will be your host?

What is my monthly budget for my online retail store?

Who will be your host?

Will I design it myself or hire out?

Do I want my website to be bold or simple?

What Payment processor works best for you?

How quick do I need to get paid?

How will you accept payment? Will you accept credit cards? Invoices? Cash? or all the above?

How can I keep my customer happy?

Is the customer, always right?

How can I keep a high response time to improve customer service?

How can I build a relationship with my customer?

When creating your packaging ask yourself, how would I like to receive my package?

What experience do you want to create for your customer?

How will you package your first sale? Where will you get your packaging supplies from?

How will you maintain your business and grow?

How can you stay motivated?

What will be my first marketing campaign?

How can I use Instagram to grow my brand?

How can I use Facebook to grow my brand?

How can I attract More followers to my IG page?

How can I get more likes on my Facebook page?

What kind of flyers will I create for my brand?

What will my Logo look like?

What is the concept for my Website?

How will I get traffic to my website?

How can I gain potential customer's trust?

Do I need models?

Will I use myself as a model?

How can I market my brand?

Will I have a grand opening?

Will I do a Grand Opening giveaway?

www.ingramcontent.com/pod-product-compliance
Lightning Source LLC
Chambersburg PA
CBHW071224220526
45468CB00002B/718